I0160918

The Book That Every Black Christian Should Read

by

Perry Khepera Kyles, Ph.D

African Diaspora Press

"An African worldview for an African world experience"

**www.adponline.info
713-900-5062**

This book is respectfully dedicated to the brothers and sisters who march onward and upward towards the light.

Other Books Published by African Diaspora Press

Classic Book Series

The Negro, by W.E.B. DuBois, 1915.
Stolen Legacy, by George G.M. James, 1954.
Wonderful Ethiopians of the Ancient Cushite Empire by Drusilla Dunjee Houston, 1926.
Walker's Appeal, by David Walker, 1830
Egyptian Ideas of the Future Life by E.A. Wallis Budge,
1899
The Kybalion, by The Three Initiates, 1908
The Egyptian Book of the Dead Translated by E.A. Wallis
Budge, 1895
Ancient Egypt: Light of the World by Gerald Massey, 1907

The Africana Studies Book Series

Egypt and Her Neighbors, edited by Michael Ogbeidi,
2011.
*Violence in God's Name: Christian and Muslim Relations
in Nigeria* by Christian Van Gorder, 2012.

The African Diaspora Lecture Series (DVD)

The African Diaspora Lecture Series is a series of public lectures given by Dr. Perry Kyles at the Eunoch Pratt Free Library in Baltimore, MD.

The series addresses the most important themes in African Diaspora History beginning with Humanity's African origins. This series utilizes a wide range of methodologies including archival materials, secondary sources, field research, genetics, and linguistics.

Topics include:

1. The African Origin of Humanity.
2. The Foundations of Nile Valley Civilization.
3. Ancient Egypt in Global Context. 4. Hannibal, Carthage, and The Punic Wars.
5. The Majesty of West African History.
6. The Origins and Impact of theMaafa.
7. Pan-Africanism and Resistance.

Table of Contents

INTRODUCTION

There are many overlooked and purposely ignored aspects regarding the origins of the Christian faith. This text was written with the intention of acquainting the Black World with the creation, evolution, and eventual devolution of Christianity. It is an interpretation and not meant to be an exhaustive treatment of the subject. Nonetheless, I stand by the conclusions drawn and encourage all inquiring minds to further investigate the subject matter for themselves. In the minds of our original Christian ancestors, true understanding can only come from within.

Chapter 1 entitled "The African Background" reveals the influences on Christianity from Ancient Egypt. It also addresses the contributions of the Gnostics who emerged in Alexandria after the fall of Ancient Egypt and the Hebrews who emerged from the region of the Red Sea.

Chapter 2, "The Historicists vs. The Salvationists" explains the core beliefs of the original Christians who I refer to in this text as "Salvationists". Also, this chapter explains the core beliefs of the "Historicists" whose values and beliefs contrasted the "Salvationists".

Chapter 3 addresses "The Roman His-Story of Christianity". The chapter illustrates how the Roman state and the Roman Catholic Church joined forces to make the "Historicist" perspective the dominant view throughout the Mediterranean.

Chapter 4 is titled "The Books Not In the Bible". It provides an analysis of some of the Gnostic and Hebrew texts that were hidden during the Roman purge of all things Salvationist. These sacred scriptures give deeper insight into the worldview of the Salvationists and the Hebrews.

Chapter 5 is "The Attack On The Ka and The BA". It also clarifies the function of race in the world of the American plantations. It reveals how this reality gave birth to destructive religious and cultural beliefs of many Africans in the Americas.

The ultimate goal of this text is to convey to my Christian brothers and sisters information that our ancestors would have considered our birthright. In the words of the ancient Christians:

> When you know yourselves then you will be known and you will understand that you are children of the living Father, but if you do not know yourselves then you live in poverty and you are poverty.
>
> *The Gospel of Thomas*

CHAPTER 1

THE AFRICAN BACKGROUND

Above. Satellite Image of the Nile River

The spiritual beliefs and cultural values of our human ancestors developed in the Highlands of Ethiopia over hundreds of thousands of years. As their knowledge and wisdom traveled down the Nile River other civilizations built on this knowledge. The first monarchy emerged in what is today the Sudan. It was called Ta-Seti, which meant "The Land of the Bows". After them came the Ancient Egyptians who established their kingdom about 5500 BCE/BC. Ancient Egypt built on the knowledge of their Nile Valley ancestors. Ancient Egyptian beliefs served as the foundation for many religions that emerged in the Old World, including Christianity and Judaism.

The Ancient Egyptians are the most successful human civilization in human history and were the spiritual leaders of the Ancient world. Even after the collapse of the Ancient Egypt, the knowledge seekers of Antiquity still looked to Egypt for guidance. Many of Egypt's teachers and learned persons migrated to Alexandria where they continued to educate the world. Alexandria, Egypt became the classroom of the whole Mediterranean world. The mythologies of the Old World, particularly the beliefs that became "religion", emerged from Egyptian spiritual concepts. To make sense of Egypt's relationship to the religions that sprang forth throughout the Mediterranean, it is essential to know the mythology of Ausar – which originated in the highlands of the Nile River.

Ausar is the most important single deity of Ancient Times and foundational to the concept of the *Crucified Savior*. Over the course of hundreds of thousands of years, there were many people with Ausar-like qualities. They were gods and goddesses on Earth, or in other words they were highly evolved beings. From the embellishment of their exploits came the mythology of Ausar - his mythology is not to be confused with *actual* history. These mythological stories were typically used to teach cultural norms.

According to the mythology, Ausar traveled the world spreading the knowledge that was not known in other parts. The world's first Resurrection Story relates to Ausar, when his brother Set cut him into fourteen different pieces. In short, it was his female compliment by the name of Auset, who

4

Ausar was recognized as the Lord of vegetation and also the Lord of the Perfect Black. He is often depicted with the crook and the flail, which symbolize the knowledge of animal and plant husbandry. According to Plutarch, a Greek scholar of Antiquity, both grapes and wine were associated with the blood of Ausar. The world's first Immaculate Conception story that we know of is associated with Ausar, his female compliment Auset, and their child Heru.

Above: The Judgment Scene from the scribe Ani's *Book of the Dead*.

Ani is being led by Anubis to have his heart weighed on the scale of MA'AT.

What is being decided is how heavy Ani's heart is, which is determined by his earthly walk. The more upright a person was in their earthly walk then the lighter their heart will be during their judgment.

Ani's heart was lighter than the feather of MA'AT. It is being recorded by Djehuti, who is the personification of wisdom. Because Ani's heart was lighter than the feather, he is accepted into the hall of Maati, or what we would call heaven. Ausar awaits him.

reassembled his body and breathed life into him. A significant aspect of this story is that the woman is a savior herself. By saving King Ausar, she also became savior of society and a savior of civilization. This contrasts the Eurocentric paradigm that we have inherited where woman is responsible for the collapse of humanity, like Eve or Pandora for example. This issue of sex and gender has been a major source of religious conflict since Greece came into the civilized world. It will surface throughout the text.

Much of what we know about Ancient Egyptian/Kemetic spiritual concepts are from *Book of Coming Forth By Day*, often referred to as *The Book Of The Dead*. To the Kemites what happens to you in the next realm of existence is determined by your actions in this realm of existence. Their conceptualization went beyond faith – it was a person's actions in this realm that determined their existence in the next realm. This is not to say that they expected perfection – they were looking at the totality of a person's earthly experience. Ultimately, it was the individual that determined the after-life experience – not another man.

The Book of the Dead, addresses the prospects of a person's entrance (in this case Ani) into the Hall of Maati. Upon that person's entrance into the Hall, they become Ausar (ex. "Ausar John Doe"). *The Book of the Dead reads*:

> Toth [the Greek name for Djehuti], the righteous judge of the great company of the

gods, who are in the presence of the god Ausar say, hear ye this judgment the heart of Ausar hath in very truth been weighed and his soul has stood as a witness for him. It had been found true by trial in the great balance there had not been found any weakness in him. He had not washed the offering in the temple, he had not done harm by his deeds, and he had uttered no evil reports while he was on Earth.

The claims are very consistent with the Forty-two Declarations, which was the moral code applied by all Kemites/Ancient Egyptians. The text continues,

the great company of the gods reply to Jehuti dwelling in Khemennu, that which cometh forth from the mouth has been ordered. Ausar: The scribe Ani triumphant, is holy and righteous, he had not sinned, neither has he done evil against us. Let it not be given to the devourer that is Ammenet, to prevail over him. Meat offerings and entrance into the presence of the god Ausar should be granted unto him together with a homestead forever in Sekhet-hetepu, as unto the followers of Heru.

Thus, he became *Ausar Ani*, himself the savior.

Ruins from an ancient Temple of Auset in Rome, Italy. Mystery schools of this type spread throughout the Mediterranean world.

After the collapse of the ancient country of Kemet and the expulsion of the Persians by the Greeks in 322 BCE, the mystery schools of the Alexandrian type spread throughout the Mediterranean Sea. The mythological teachings associated with Alexandria originated in the heartland of Africa. These religious cults spread from Alexandria to the whole of the Mediterranean. Ancestor George G.M. James stated in his book *Stolen Legacy* that the Egyptian mystery schools were based on the religious beliefs of Memphis, an Ancient Egyptian city. This belief system is called the *Memphite Theology*. Sources of African and European literature verify this fact. The *Memphite theology* emphasized:

> the deification of man and taught that the soul of man, if liberated from its bodily fetters, could enable him to be god like and see the gods in this life.

This belief system recognized humanity's inner divinity and also human potential once liberated from bodily fetters. From this belief system came the belief system that we today call Christianity.

The people that we generally refer to as "Gnostics" were the earliest practitioners of Christianity. The word "gnosis" means "to know" in Greek. Gnostics placed great value on the acquisition of knowledge. To them, study enabled a person to develop what we call "divine intuition", to become an exalted being, and ultimately to transcend the fetters of the world. Their beliefs were foundational to our very first Christian ancestors as the religion began to emerge. The Gnostics were hugely influential in the spiritual and intellectual world of Ancient Alexandria in Egypt.

Another influential group of African ancestors were the Hebrews. The Hebrews spiritual and physical presence was prominent in the Ancient Mediterranean world. By Hebrew we mean those whose genetic and cultural ancestors were ancient "Canaanites" that migrated from the Red Sea into the Mediterranean world. They were Black. Ancient Egyptian spirituality was at the root of their religion. From the Hebrews comes the word "*Christ*". This term *Christos* was used as early as the third century BCE, when it appears in a Hebrew spiritual text that was called *The Septuagint*. The Septuagint was translated from Hebrew to Greek. The word Christ comes from the Greek word "*christos*", which means "anointed". An anointing can confer divine power to an individual or an object. For example, one could anoint a shield or a sword going into battle, or a person to prepare them for a particular task. Thus the word signified a title and not a name at least 300 years before the time that the Historicists say that Jesus Christ was born.

Above: Script from the Septuagint Bible. The term "Christ" was used as early as the 3rd century BCE in the translation of the Hebrew Old Testament into Greek.

Chapter 2

The Historicists vs. The Salvationists

The Historicist belief that an individual has to go through one of the church intermediaries to get to Jesus who is also God is still with us today. The Historicist belief was the minority perspective within the Christian world all the way up until 200 CE (AD). This perspective is called the "historicist" perspective because they argued that Jesus Christ was an actual, real, historical figure that existed on Earth. The Historicists took Jesus' resurrection story literally. They argued that the only path to salvation was through faith in Jesus' sacrifice. Again, as far as the multitudes were concerned, the Historicist perspective was on the margins and only gained numbers with the backing of Roman military might. The dominant perspective among the Christians was the "Salvationist" perspective. They did not argue that Jesus was an actual human being, that Jesus came in human form, or that he was birthed by a human. The Salvationists believed that the savior's resurrection should not be taken literally but allegorically. They insisted that humanity has the potential to obtain *gnosis*, which is *divine intuition*.

The Salvationists were not a monolithic group but comprised of several "schools". One of the best known of these groups were the "Therapeuts", who were headquartered in Alexandria – their name means "physician of the soul". They were healers and one of their common prescriptions was strict dietary discipline. They were a savior-cult who thought of the savior as "the light of the world that every eye can see". Their beliefs conflicted greatly with the Historicist perspective.

Philo's commentary is helpful on this subject. He was an adult when Jesus was supposed to have been born and he lived for a significant time after Jesus was supposedly born. Philo was a prolific historian, but never mentioned Jesus one time in his writings. Philo said about the Therapeuts, "they possess also short works by early writers, the founders of their sect who left man specimens of the *allegorical* method". Thus the stories were designed to deliver a special meaning or special idea with the use of metaphors.

Some of the Gnostics of Alexandria thought of matter as evil. They believed that salvation can only come through Gnosis, which was esoteric knowledge of spiritual truth that was backed by earthly deeds and dietary discipline. In 1945 in the heartland of Egypt, papyri papers named the *Nag Hammadi* were found. They were hidden in the early centuries of the CE (AD) era and were not found until 1945. They were hidden because the Romans began to murder in high numbers those who did not adopt their Historicist position.

The Historicists took a starkly different perspective. Justin Martyr is a good starting point for the Historicist perspective. He wrote in the 2nd century CE. He was among the most influential of writers that accepted the reincarnation of Jesus as literal. Martyr wrote that:

> Isiah did not send you to the back to wash away murder and other sins which all of the water of the ocean could not cleanse, but by faith through the blood and the death of Christ who suffered death for this precise purpose.

Thus Justin Martyr promoted the notion that a person's sins were washed away by faith that Jesus Christ suffered for their sins. In another passage, he commented:

> We assert that the word, our teacher Jesus Christ was not born as the result of sexual relations and that he was crucified and rose and ascended to heaven, we propose nothing new or different from that which you say of the so called sons of Jupiter.

Martyr wrote from the Historicist perspective at a time when Romans practiced a number of different religions, including its traditional pagan religion. He compared his belief in Jesus Christ with the Roman deity Jupiter in an effort to legitimize his beliefs in the eyes of non-believers.

The Hebrews is a cultural/linguistic group that has played a major part in the milieu of the Ancient world. Their identity has been assumed by the people we today call Jews. The Jews of today are largely comprised of a group from Turkey called the Ashkenazi. They assumed the identity of the Hebrews about 800 CE/AD. The Hebrews were clearly of African descent as shown by linguistic studies. Linguistics proves that the Hebrew language originated in Ethiopia, along with Arabic and Meta Neter (Ancient Egyptian language). The Hebrews were not passivists like most of the Gnostics were. The Hebrews were unwilling to pay taxes and unlike most of the Gnostics, they were willing to slay their enemies. Among their enemies were the Romans. There is an incredibly useful primary source called *The Dead Sea Scrolls*. Within this resource is a passage called "The War Scrolls". "The War Scrolls" call for the death of the sons of Japheth. According to Bible mythology, the sons of Japheth are the Europeans. Thus the beliefs of the Hebrews were consistent with most Gnostics in that they do not believe that a man named Jesus Christ was immaculately conceived and do not believe that he will appear as a savior. It is important to remember that they differ from the Gnostics in their willingness to use violence.

Without the military influence of Rome the Historicist perspective would have remained a perpetual joke amongst Christians.

Chapter 3

The Roman His-Story of Christianity

Mythology is the best method of understanding the values of a culture. The Romans' story of their origin is the story of two baby brothers by the name of Remus and Romulus.

Rhea, the mother of Remus and Romulus, was raped and gave birth to the twins. To prevent the two boys from being murdered, they were floated down a river in a basket and eventually raised by a wolf.

Misogyny is reflected in the myth and also in the culture of the imperialist Romans. Misogyny is reflected in the Roman version of Christianity that they eventually forced on their subjects.

The worldview of the Romans can best be explained with the use of the *Two Cradle Theory*. According to the *Two Cradle Theory* there is a contrast between two different cultural paths. This theory was popularized by Cheikh Diop and elaborated on by Dr. Charles Finch. However the first people to articulate the contrast of these two cradles were the Kemites/Ancient Egyptians. From their perspective, the inhumanity practiced by Northern Cradle cultures was a consequence of their origin in barren lands. The Romans came into existence from the Northern Cradle culture, which was typified by misogyny, perpetual anxiety, and the whole idea that wealth and resources are finite. Thusly, they proceeded as if the advancement of others meant the decline of their own society. The Northern Cradle cultures had been devolving for about 40,000 years before Rome was established.

Initially the Roman Empire, was preoccupied with "empire" and taxation, not religion. There were many people that the Romans despised, however the Romans tolerated them as long as they paid taxes. The failure to pay their taxes made the Romans feel that the Hebrews had to reigned in. Dozens of religions were practiced throughout the empire and in Rome, as exemplified for the Temple of Auset (above). As the groups like the Gnostics, the Therapeuts, and the Hebrews started to create a greater problem for the Romans. The Romans decided that the state needed to take a stronger stance on the religion issue and create a much greater degree of uniformity. This objective of uniformity was behind the church rhetoric that many still today accept as absolute truth.

The bastard version of Christianity that was created by the Historicists, and promoted by the Romans, hinged on the claim that Paul *met* Jesus. This claim is fallacious. The Romans *created* Paul and borrowed from a number of existing spiritual texts to support the Historicist perspective. In several of the hidden spiritual texts you see the similarities, but also the passages that were problematic to the Romans. We do not have any evidence that anyone in the *Bible* existed. To make matters worse we have evidence of people who lived thousands of years before Jesus was born, yet no evidence of one single person from the *Bible*. That is one more reason that I am more inclined to go with the Salvationists as oppose to the Historicist perspective.

Paul was supposedly a Jewish citizen of Rome. We are told by Historicists that Paul actually met the resurrected Jesus. Let us read Paul's supposed interaction with Jesus as it appears in "Acts" of the *KJV*:

> And Saul [Paul], yet breathing out threatenings and slaughter against the disciples of the Lord, went unto the high priest. And desired of him letters to Damascus to the synagogues, that if he found any of this way, whether they were men or women, he might bring them bound

unto Jerusalem. And as he journeyed, he came near Damascus: and suddenly there shined round about him a light from heaven. And he fell to the Earth, and heard a voice saying unto him, "Saul, Saul, why persecutest thou me?" And he said, "Who art thou, Lord?" And the Lord said, "I am Jesus whom thou persecute: it is hard for thee to kick against the pricks".

Acts 9 (*King James Version*)

Here Paul is talking to somebody that exists in heaven; he is talking to someone in the sky. He is not talking to someone who is here in the earthly realm. Did Paul meet Jesus first hand? No he did not – and neither did anyone else. What has made it so easy to cast this as an absolute truth is the prevalence of illiteracy among subjugated peoples throughout the world and the use of violence against non-believers.

A common question that students have had through my years of teaching at the collegiate level is "How were the Europeans able to defeat the Africans?" "Were they better fighters?" My response is usually something like "99% of the time, it is somebody that looks like you on the other side of the battlefield." What has made the expansion of White Supremacy possible is the cooperation of members of the group that is under attack. The Roman colonization of northern Africa was no different. The power of the Romans was strengthened by the Africans that were agents of the Roman Empire. One of them was named Tertullian. He was an agent of the

Catholic Church and the Roman Empire. He was born in 155 CE in Carthage, Africa. Imagine what Carthage would have been like if the Carthaginians under Hannibal Barca had not lost to the Romans in the Punic Wars that took place between Rome and Carthage. However, when the Carthaginians gave up those fertile islands in the Mediterranean and the land of Carthage itself, the Europeans gained access to Africa's greatest minds - one destructive result of integration. It was Tertullian that made Latin the language of the church. He traveled the Mediterranean world proselytizing and spreading the word of God as he knew it. He is credited for being a very versatile, well-trained scholar. By serving Rome, he was essentially a Black man in the service of white supremacy. Tertullian is quoted as having said:

> For you do know what you should know, your faith save thee. Not your biblical learning, faith is established in the Rule, to know nothing against the Rule, is to know everything.

This motivated and determined African proselytized the Historicist position that advanced the interests of the Roman Empire and the Catholic Church.

Another determined African that advanced the position of Rome was Septimus Severus - he was also Carthaginian. He ascended in the Roman army and eventually became the Roman Emperor. He then issued a law in 202 CE declaring that there was to be no more conversion to Christianity or Judaism. He turned a deaf ear as Historicist mobs slaughtered innocent Salvationists. As anyone can clearly see by the contributions of Tertullian, Septimius Severus, and countless other Blacks – Rome could not have prevailed in Africa without the complicity of Africans.

There were several Africans who fought the good fight to preserve the Salvationist perspective. The African priest Arius held firm to his belief even with his life on the line at the Nicaea Council. The Council of Nicaea was convened by the Roman Emperor Constantine to bring uniformity to the Christian Church. By 324 CE Constantine had united the eastern and western Catholic Church. He fought under the banner of Christianity and thus the Historicist perspective officially became the state religion. What he wanted to do was bring uniformity to the church, but his primary issue was with the teachings of an Alexandrian priest named Arius. It was at the Council of Nicaea, which convened in contemporary Turkey, that the position that Jesus came in the physical form was institutionalized by the state. From that point onward the Roman state intensified their efforts to marginalize and destroy the Salvationist perspective, and all others who opposed their position. To the contrary Arius' position was that:

> Were he in the truest sense a son, he must have come after the Father, therefore the time obviously was when he was not, and hence he was a finite being.

This contrasted the position that Jesus was "the Father, the Son, and the Holy Spirit". Arius carried influence with others in the priesthood. In his efforts to neutralize Arius, Constantine declared:

> ... if any writing composed by Arius should be found, it should be handed over to the flame, so that not only will the evil of his teachings be obliterated but nothing will be left to remind anyone of him, and I hereby make a public order, if anyone has been discovered to have hidden a writing composed by Arius and not to have immediately brought it forward and destroyed it by fire, his penalty shall be death. As soon as he is discovered in this offense he shall be submitted for capital punishment.

As seen above, the Romans went to drastic measures to vanquish the early Christian perspective that Arius maintained.

The violence factor is often overlooked by students of religion. Violence is the game-changer that has been employed by the spiritual and intellectual inferiors of the world. The violence was often physical, mental, and spiritual. Black Wall Street in Tulsa, OK is a good example. They were self-sufficient, which is the first step to establishing stability. However they could not defend their community against the violence of their spiritual inferiors. The only reason the Historicist won out over the Salvationist was the violence factor. Violence has been the most important factor in the acceptance of fiction as truth.

As the Historicist perspective prevailed in the Roman alliance of church and state, spiritual life was reduced to only that which was consistent with the doctrine of the Roman state. For example, in 392 CE a Roman emperor by the name of Theodosius exhorted:

> We command that those persons who follow this rule shall embrace the name of Catholic Christians. The rest, however, whom we adjudge demented and insane, shall sustain the infamy of heretical dogmas. Their meeting places shall not receive the name of churches, and they shall be smitten first by divine vengeance and secondly by the retributions of our own initiative, which we shall assume in accordance with the divine judgment. We command that all their fanes, temples, and shrines, if even now any remain entire, shall be destroyed by the command of magistrates and shall be purified by the erection of the sign of the venerable Christian religion.

So this is how Christianity became white, how Blacks became cursed, and how women created sin.

Hypatia was an Alexandrian priestess of the Gnostic type. She was an exceedingly accomplished scholar of her day as was her father before her.

The Serapeum was a temple built in honor of the deity Serapis. It was established in the 3rd century BCE as an extension of the Royal Library of Alexandria. In 391 CE, fanatical Historicist Christians burned the Serapeum to the ground.

Henceforth misogyny typified the doctrine and the practices of the clergy. As I have often stated, European misogyny has been destructive for human civilization in general. The Catholic Church was willing to destroy great talents and contributors to society in order to reinforce patriarchy. Among these great talents was the Alexandrian priestess Hypatia. She was a very popular teacher and was particularly strong in the areas of mathematics and astronomy. She had a huge following, was highly respected, and maintained involvement in political matters of the day. Her life was put in jeopardy when she challenged the Roman bishop of Alexandria by the name of Cyril. In 415 CE Cyril had his followers take this woman from her chariot, beat her, and carve the skin off her body with clam shells.

The wretched alliance of church and state also insisted on the destruction of all literature that undermined the Historicist doctrine. In 391 the foremost library in the world at that time called the Serapeum was burned to the ground at the hands of Historicist Christian fanatics. Hundreds of Salvationist schools were closed and their monuments were destroyed. One 5th century church official boasted:

> Every trace of the old philosophy and literature of a ancient world has been vanished from the face of the Earth.

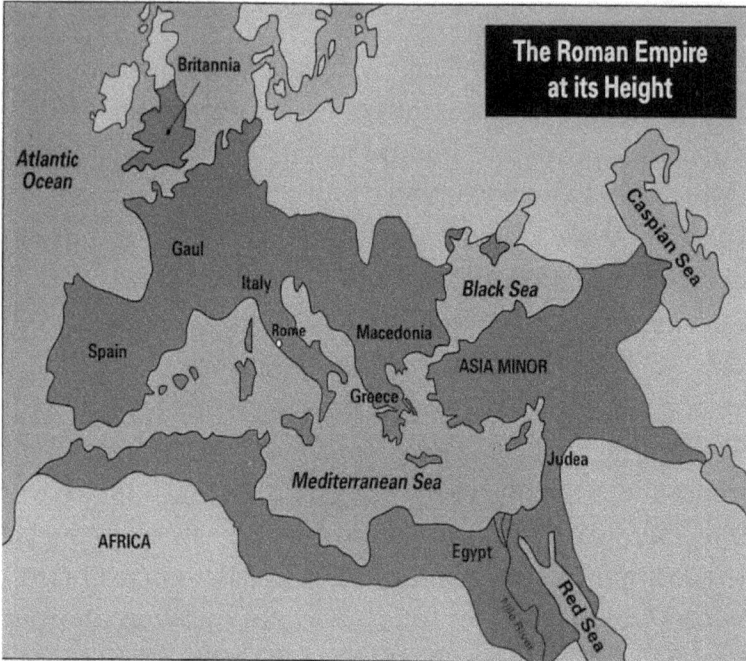

The Roman Empire at its height.

The Salvationist perspective had been dominant until the 2nd Century CE/AD. The Historicist perspective, despite being built on lies, overtook the Salvationist perspective with the backing of force and deceit. They borrowed from many of the sacred writings and modified them to suit their purpose. Thus was the function of the fictional character Paul.

Salvationists were forced to either hide or destroy their literature. In recent years several of the books that they hid have come to light.

Chapter 4

The Books Not In the Bible

There are sixty six books in the *King James Bible*. There are also hundreds of books that did not make it into that text. Here I will familiarize you with several of the texts that escaped the torches of the Historicist mobs.

I will draw from the groupings of ancient texts that were hidden by Hebrews and Salvationists as the wicked alliance of the Roman state and the Catholic Church applied pressure to con-conformists. The first text that I will address will be the *Gospel of Mary*, which was first found in Lower Egypt in 1896. Lower Egypt is the region closer to the Mediterranean. This papyrus was purchased in 1896 by Dr. Carl Reinhardt in Cairo, Egypt and then taken to Berlin. There are millions of valuable artifacts such as this one that are in personal collections and in museums throughout the western world. The second is *The Dead Sea Scrolls*, which were first found twelve miles east of Jerusalem in caves along the Dead Sea in 1947. Lastly, I will draw on the striking passages in the *Nag Hammadi* papyri, which was first found in Upper Egypt (the highlands) in 1945.

The message of *The Gospel of Mary* was not consistent with the patriarchal religious culture within the Roman Empire. A series of passages will clearly illustrate this:

> The Savior said, All nature, all formations, all creatures exist in and with one another, and they will be resolved again into their own roots.

Note the scientific nature of this interpretation. This was inconsistent with Peter's beliefs. The text continues:

> Peter said, Since you have explained everything to us, tell us this also: What is the sin of the world?
> The Savior said *There is no sin, but it is you who make sin when you do the things that are like the nature of adultery, which is called sin* [emphasis added].
>
> That is why the Good came into your midst, to the essence of every nature in order to restore it to its root.

Thus, according to the Gospel of Mary, there is no original sin and the nature of all things is good.

> Then he continued and said, That is why you become sick and die, for you are deprived of the one who can heal you.
> He who has a mind to understand, let him understand.

Matter gave birth to a passion that has no
equal, which proceeded from something
contrary to nature. Then there arises a
disturbance in its whole body.
He who has ears to hear, let him hear.
*Beware that no one lead you astray saying Lo
here or lo there! For the Son of Man is within
you* [emphasis added].
Follow after Him!
Those who seek Him will find Him.

Thus the only way to heel sickness is from within the
self. The emphasized lines are similar to Luke 17:21 in
the *King James Bible*. The *KJV* says "the kingdom of
God is within you", however the *Gospel of Mary* says
"the son of man is within you". This relates directly to
the Gnostic belief that you become the crucified
savior as oppose to you relying on an actual person
named Jesus to reappear. The passage continues:

Peter said to Mary, Sister we know that the
Savior loved you more than the rest of the
woman. Tell us the words of the Savior which
you remember which you know, but we do not,
nor have we heard them.

Mary responded:

The first form is darkness, the second desire,
the third ignorance, the fourth is the
excitement of death, the fifth is the kingdom of

31

the flesh, the sixth is the foolish wisdom of flesh, and the seventh is the wrathful wisdom. These are the seven powers of wrath.

Peter had a negative response to this:

> Did He really speak privately with a woman and not openly to us? Are we to turn about and all listen to her? Did he prefer her to us?

Here Peter appeals to the patriarchy, but with failed results. Levi, a male supporter of Mary, interjects to say:
> Now I see you contending against the woman like the adversaries. But if the Savior made her worthy, who are you indeed to reject her? Surely the Savior knows her very well...

The texts reflect the value system of the Christians who saw fit to hide them under threat of them being found by the patriarchy. In this mythological allegory, Mary was valued for wisdom be even the males that searched for "The Son of Man".

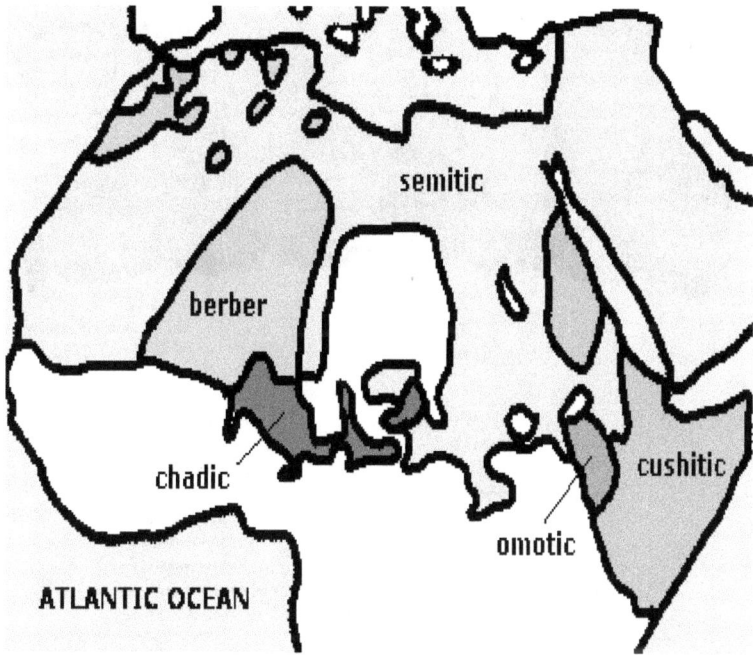

Linguistics tell us that the Hebrews were a part of the Ethiopic language family, which originated in Ethiopia. Hebrew, Arabic, the Meta Neter, and a number of other languages in that region all originated from Ethiopia.

These Hebrews had an African genotype and African phenotype. In time they mixed with foreigners as did many of the original inhabitants of the Mediterranean world.

Dead Sea Scroll Text Written In Hebrew.

Twelve miles east of Jerusalem in what we today call Israel, the largest cache of *Dead Sea Scrolls* were found in the caves above.

In the case of the Hebrews, it was their reluctance to pay taxes that raised the ire of the Romans. The Hebrews were contemptuous of Roman culture. This enmity grew as the Hebrews refused to accept Jesus Christ as *the* Savior. To them Jesus Christ was simply a prophet, but had never been and never would be *the* Savior. Consequently several Hebrew populations were dislocated from Rome (63CE) and Israel (70 CE and 135 CE). Some of them hid their texts in caves for preservation.

Within the *Dead Sea Scrolls* is a particular text called "The War Scrolls". This scroll gives insight into the beliefs and values of the Hebrews:

> At the beginning of the undertaking of the sons of light, they shall start against the lot of the sons of darkness.....The sons of Levi, the sons of Judah, and the exiles of the desert, shall fight against them and their forces...when the exiles of the sons of light return from the desert....and here shall be great tumult against the sons of Japheth....

They considered their enemy to be the sons of Japheth, who are the Europeans and the Romans in particular. *The War Scroll* continues:

> When they draw near to the battle shall write on their standards The Right Hand of God, The Assembly of God, The Panic of God, The Slain of God.

The Hebrews dwelled on the moral shortcomings of the Romans and the other sons of Japheth. "The War Scroll" makes it clear that the Hebrews were anticipating a day of reckoning for the sons Japheth. This explains the Roman attacks on the Hebrews in Rome, Israel, and Alexandria, and also why the scrolls were hidden.

Humanity's effort to preserve their most ancient secrets and their highest knowledge in print has been maintained by griots over the course of thousands of years. Of this group the Gnostics are worthy of special recognition due to their unwavering effort to pass down esoteric knowledge. Their intellectual leadership from 200 BCE/BC – 200 CE/AD is the reason why we are today able to clearly understand the lineage of Christianity's most ancient beliefs. Gnostics were influential particularly in Alexandria but also throughout the Mediterranean. Their belief system was consistent with the core beliefs of our ancient Shemsu Heru ancestors that emerged out of Ethiopia. The concept of "gnosis" emphasized humanity's potential to spiritually align itself with The Most High and to live free of the world's fetters.

After 1945 scholars began to translate the Nag Hammadi writings. Some of the Nag Hammadi material is quite similar to passages in the *KJV Bible* and the parts that challenged the beliefs of the Historicists were not passed down to be included in the *KJV*. Here are a few passages from the *Nag Hammadi* that are relevant to this discussion:

Jesus said, if your leader say to you, look the Father's kingdom is the sky, then the birds will precede you, if they say to you it is in the sea, then the fish will precede you, rather the Father's kingdom is within you and it is outside of you. "The Gospel of Thomas" from *The Nag Hammadi Papers.*

Note the similarity of this text to Luke 17:12 in the *KJV Holy Bible*. This passage from the *Gospel of Thomas* goes on to say:

When you know yourselves then you will be known and you will understand that you are children of the living Father, but if you do not know yourselves then you live in poverty and you are poverty.

This passage contradicted the party line of the Roman state and the Roman Catholic Church. The Roman had two primary policies on subjugated people: that they pay their taxes and also that they accept the Roman bishops as intermediaries to the Almighty.

There are other examples of scripture from the *Nag Hammadi* that contradict the Historicist perspective:

When you see one who is not born of woman, fall on your faces and worship, that is your father.   From "The Gospel of Thomas"

However the Historicists argue that Jesus was literally born of woman; thus this scripture is in complete contradiction to the Historicists. I continue:

> Since the perfection of the All is in the Father, it is necessary for the All to ascend to him. Therefore if one has knowledge, he gets what belongs to him and draws it to himself. For him who is ignorant is deficient and it is a great deficiency since he lacked that which will make him perfect. from "The Gospel of Truth" in *The Nag Hammadi*

Note that this passage addresses humanity's potential as perfection, as oppose to innate sinfulness or being born in sin. The passage continues:

> Since the perfection of the all is in the Father, it is necessary for the all to ascend to him and for each one to get the things which are his. He registered them first having prepared them to be given to them that came from him.
> From "Gospel of Truth"

This passage suggests that plentitude is the destiny of humanity. Also note the emphasis on the Almighty (the All) instead of the intermediary. At the core of Gnosticism is the belief that a person will become *Ausar, the Father*, or *the Crucified Savior*. In contrast, the Roman concept emphasized intermediaries such as the "historical" Jesus Christ or church bishops. Ironic when we think about white missionaries "civilizing" Africans to no longer worship local dieties or ancestors.

Over the course of the past one hundred years dozens of sacred texts have been found and translated. Most were translated from the African languages of Hebrew or Coptic. Together they reveal the *true* beliefs and values of our Christian ancestors.

Chapter 5

The Attack on the Ka and the BA

There were several spiritual concepts that were destroyed after the Roman/European colonization of Africa and the Americas. Among those are the two Kemetic spiritual concepts above.

The Ka (to the left) symbolizes the universal part of humanity - that part of us that is linked us to the whole of the universe.

The Ba (to the right) represents the uniqueness in each human.

The Historicists' best weapon was violence - both physical and psychological. With its use the Romans expanded their empire throughout the Mediterranean basin. This included Africa, Asia, and Europe. In its wake lay a number of spiritual concepts that have existed since our emergence here on Earth 1,000,000 years ago. The major spiritual concepts that threatened the Roman Empire were that:

1. Humanity is divine. Spiritually and anatomically linked to the power of the Most High Almighty.
2. Humanity's nature is exaltation – not sin. It derives from the harmony between the spiritual and the physical.
3. Sin could be overcome by drawing on "The Father", "Ausar", "Crucified Savior" that exists within you.
4. Deities represent aspects of energy forces that emanate from the Almighty. They explain the realms between the Almighty and our existence on the physical plane.

The tsunami of rape, pillage, and slavery by the Romans served as a blueprint for the European colonizers of the Americas – themselves former colonial subjects of the Roman Empire. However what made slavery in the Americas different from slavery throughout the Mediterranean was the preoccupation with race, as the economic structures of the Americas required a suitable social reality to insure its existence. Racism provided the necessary social apparatus to ensure the perpetuation of an inhumane economic system.

Essential to the strategy of racism as it has been practiced in the Americas was the internalization of racism by subjugated peoples. European colonizers became aware of the deeply spiritual nature of their subjects. Thus, the physical threats were backed with a message of eternal damnation for non–acquiescence. Over the course of the last 600 years American Africans have had the Historicist perspective forced upon them, as opposed to the Salvationist perspective of our ancestors who created Christianity. Through those Historicist teachings, they began the attack on the *ka* and *ba* of all enslaved and colonized people.

Catechism books were used as instruction books on how to teach the Historicist perspective. They were produced by the church and the objective was to teach their followers/teachers how to teach the religion of Christianity to non-followers. Most of the time, it was used by a person who read English to teach Christianity to people that did not read English. One of these books was called *A Catechism of Scripture, Doctrine, and Practice; Designed Also for the Oral Instruction of Colored Persons*, 1837. One passage from the book implores:

> Servants be obedient to them that are masters...as unto Christ...doing the will of God from the heart...

> Servants be subject to your masters with all fear...not only to the good and gentle but to the froward. But if ye do well and suffer for it ye take it patiently, this acceptable to God...

> Ephesians 5-8, *King James Version*

Thus subservience to the slave masters became the will of God and entrance into heaven was only possible through the acceptance of such beliefs. The catechism book continued:

Q. How many Gods are there?
  A. There is only one living and true God. Deut. 6:4

Q. How many persons are there in the Godhead?
  A. Three

Q. What are their names?
  A. The Father, the Son, and the Holy Ghost?

Q. How do we certainly know this?

A. *The Bible tells us so* [emphasis added]

As a consequence of the Historicist perspective being forced on our ancestors, there are today a multitude of Black Christians who are steadfastly convinced that a white historical Jesus walked the Earth.

As for the Africans who lived through the ordeal of slavery, no aspect of their lives was untouched by white supremacy – least of all their spiritual life. On holidays it was common for white preachers to address the slave community. That sermon would go as such:

> Well darkies, I am happy to see so many shining eyes, and greasy faces today...through the economy of God's grace you transplanted upon American soil...through much toil on the part of the white man, you are becoming quite intelligent...The white man...has not only imparted you to his straight hair, high nose, blue eyes, thin lips, and perfect form...it is to be hoped that you have a soul...by his care and attention, and your obedience to his precepts stand a great chance to be admitted upon the ground floor of God's glorious temple in heaven...
>
> white preacher, Reverend Policy, in Georgia

One slave is quoted as having said:

> Slavery in this...was a godsend....if it had not been for the slave traffic, we would still be living in Africa. I would be a heathen and my children would be heathen. Out of bad comes good...

> ...the Lord made three nations, the white, the red and the black... those black ignoramuses in Africa forgot God, and didn't have no religion and God blessed and prospered the white people that did remember him...

Thus the degraded collective position of Africans throughout the world is largely due to the physical and psychological damage done to the *ka* and the *ba*. Africans must be at the center of their own value system. Our standard of beauty should be decidedly African. Our actions should be designed to progress *us* as opposed to the Eurocentric world as the Historicist position has been used to do.

Closing

We could study for a lifetime the extent to which the Historicists have pulled the wool over the eyes of many ancestors and the current multitudes of the world. It emerged from the Roman efforts to rule efficiently and the subsequent effort of other groups to rule by depriving their subjects of knowledge and freedom. Thought is the root of action and free thought, as well as free will, is the God-given privilege of all humanity. This is to say that we have to shake off the inferiority complex and negative assumptions of our brothers and sisters – both stem from *plantation socialization*.

It is time for all God's chosen people to assume our rightful place on this Earth. Gnosis is God's will, however a balance must be maintained between our earthly and our spiritual lives. The ancient Gnostics were unbalanced and could not defend their own priests such as Hypatia and Arius. Those of us who have been chosen to manifest here in the physical realm must learn from the tribulations of our ancestors and respond accordingly. The Sons and Daughters of Light must fulfill their earthly destiny despite the challenges that lie before them. This can happen with liberation from the subconscious belief that we are born in sin and that our bodies typify sin. Humanity is born divine – not in sin.

As for we Black Christians, we must teach the values that are designed to bring us closer to a state of gnosis such as the following core beliefs of our ancestors:

1) Humanity is divine. Spiritually and anatomically linked to the power of the Most High Almighty.

2) Humanity's nature is exaltation – not sin. It derives from the harmony between the spiritual and the physical.

3) Sin could be overcome by drawing on "The Father", "Ausar", "Crucified Savior" that exists within you.

4) Deities represent aspects of energy forces that emanate from the Almighty. They explain the realms between the Almighty and our existence on the physical plane.

Neither shall they say, Lo here! or, lo there! for, behold, the kingdom of God is within you.

Luke 17:21 *KJV*

Jesus said, If your leaders say to you, 'Look, the (Father's) kingdom is in the sky,' then the birds of the sky will precede you. If they say to you, 'It is in the sea,' then the fish will precede you. Rather, the (Father's) kingdom is within you and it is outside you.

The Gospel of Thomas

Suggested Readings

Yosef ben-Jochannan, *African Origins of the Major Western Religions*

E.A. Wallis Budge (translator), *The Egyptian Book of the Dead*

Millar Burrows, *The Dead Sea Scrolls*

George James, *Stolen Legacy*

Karen King, *What Is Gnosticism*

Perry Kyles, *Kemet 101: An Introduction to Ancient Egyptian History and Culture*

Tim Leedom, *The Book Your Church Doesn't Want You To Read*

Acharya S, *The Christ Conspiracy*

The Three Initiates, *The Kybalion*

Walter Williams, *The History of Christianity*

Dr. Perry Khepera Kyles

Presents

The Ancient Egypt Sacred Lands Tour

December 23, 2014 – January 4, 2015

$ 3,500 – All Inclusive

Above: The Giza Plateau featuring the Great Pyramid, Heru em Akhet a.k.a. the Sphinx, and the Step Pyramid that was designed by the great genius Imhotep.

The all-inclusive trip includes: round trip air fare from New York to Cairo, deluxe hotel accommodations, breakfast and dinner every day (lunch on five days), entrance into all monuments and temples, presentations by Dr. Kyles at the hotels and the monuments, boat rides, party at Nubian Village, and much more.

For information or an application please contact Dr. Kyles at 832-322-4032, e-mail at tours@drkyles.com or visit www.drkyles.com

www.ingramcontent.com/pod-product-compliance
Lightning Source LLC
Chambersburg PA
CBHW060557100426
42742CB00013B/2594